Science Vocabulary Readers

Fantastic Fish

Elizabeth Bennett

SCHOLASTIC INC.

NEW YORK • TORONTO • LONDON • AUCKLAND • SYDNEY
MEXICO CITY • NEW DELHI • HONG KONG • BUENOS AIRES

ISBN-13: 978-0-545-06081-3 / ISBN-10: 0-545-06081-8

Photo Credits:
Cover © Jeff Hunter/Getty Images; title page: © American Images/Getty Images; contents page, from top: © Pete Atkinson/Getty Images, © Don Farrell/Getty Images, © Hal Beral/Image Quest Marine; page 4: © Pete Atkinson/Getty Images; page 5: © Dorling Kindersley/Getty Images; page 5, inset: © John Foxx/Getty Images; page 6, top left: © Reinhard/ARCO/Nature Picture Library; page 6, top right: © Jane Burton/Nature Picture Library; page 6, bottom left: © Tim Martin/Nature Picture Library; page 6, bottom right: © Gerard Lacz/Animals Animals; page 7, top left: © Jeff Rotman/Nature Picture Library; page 7, top right: © Georgette Douwma/Getty Images; page 7, bottom left: © Fred Bavendam/Minden Pictures; page 7, bottom right: © Brandon Cole Photography/Nature Picture Library; page 8: © Don Farrell/Getty Images; page 9: © Wolcott Henry/Getty Images: page 9, inset: © Jeff Rotman/Nature Picture Library; page 10: © Georgette Douwma/Getty Images; page 11, left: © Georgette Douwma/Getty Images; page 11, right: © Flip Nicklin/Minden Pictures; page 12: © Hal Beral/Image Quest Marine; page 12, inset: © Davies and Starr/Getty Images; page 13: © Georgette Douwma/Getty Images; page 13, inset: © John Foxx/Getty Images; page 14, top left: © David Gotshall/Getty Images; page 14, top right: © Georgette Douwma/Getty Images; page 14, middle left: © Fred Bavendam/Minden Pictures; page 14, bottom left: © Norbert Wu/Minden Pictures; page 14, bottom right: © David Hall/Nature Picture Library; page 15: © Panoramic Images/Getty Images; back cover: © Stephen Frink/Getty Images.

Photo research by Dwayne Howard
Design by Holly Grundon

Copyright © 2009 by Lefty's Editorial Services
All rights reserved. Published by Scholastic Inc.

SCHOLASTIC and associated logos are trademarks and/or registered trademarks of Scholastic Inc.

12 11 10 9 8 7 6 5   9 10 11 12 13 14/0

Printed in the U.S.A.
First printing, January 2009

Contents

Chapter 1
Meet the Fish

Page 4

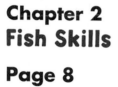

Chapter 2
Fish Skills

Page 8

Chapter 3
Amazing Fish

Page 12

Glossary and Comprehension Questions
Page 16

Meet the Fish

Fast Fact

Fish have been around for more than 450 million years.

What kind of animals are right at home in the water? The answer is fish!

Fish Parts

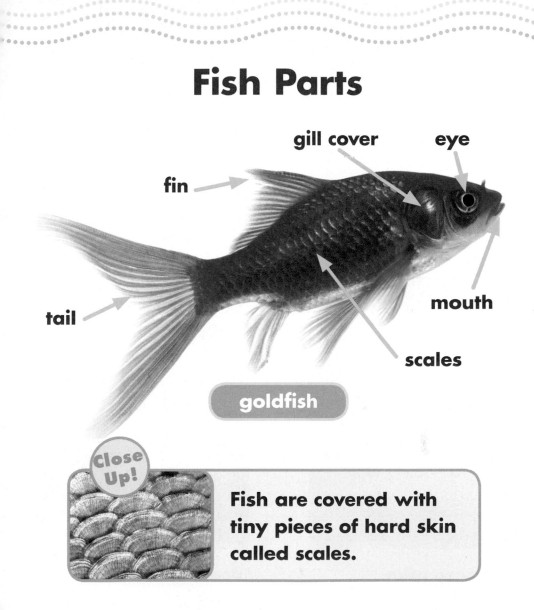

gill cover

eye

fin

tail

mouth

scales

goldfish

Close Up!

Fish are covered with tiny pieces of hard skin called scales.

What makes a fish a fish? Fish have **fins** and tails for swimming. They also have **gills** for getting oxygen from the water so they can breathe.

Freshwater Fish

brook trout

catfish

northern pike

black bass

Different fish live in different places. Some live in rivers, streams, brooks, lakes, and ponds. This kind of water is called **freshwater**.

Saltwater Fish

swordfish

angelfish

clownfish

great white shark

Some fish live in the ocean. This kind of water is called **saltwater** because it contains salt. There are even some fish that can live in both freshwater and saltwater.

Chapter 2

Fish Skills

Fast Fact

Fish sleep with their eyes open!

black moor goldfish

How do fish survive in the water? They use their **senses**! Most fish have one eye on each side of their heads. This helps them watch out for predators.

Sharks can smell a drop of blood that is one-quarter mile away.

A lizardfish swallows another fish whole.

Most fish have a good sense of smell. This helps them find food. Different fish eat different things. Some munch on plants. Some eat other fish.

surgeonfish

Fast Fact

Some schools have more than 200,000 fish in them.

Many fish travel in groups called **schools**. Why? There is safety in numbers. A little fish in a big group has a better chance of surviving a predator's attack.

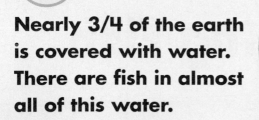

Fast Fact

Nearly 3/4 of the earth is covered with water. There are fish in almost all of this water.

1/4 = land

3/4 = water

Golden damsels live in warm water.

Polar cod live in frigid water.

Some fish live in warm water. Other fish live in cold water. But guess what? Their bodies stay the same temperature as the water around them.

Chapter 3

Amazing Fish

dwarf goby

Close Up!

A dwarf goby looks like this close up. In real life, it could fit on a penny.

Fish come in all shapes and sizes. Some are itsy-bitsy. This one is about the size of a grain of rice.

whale shark

Fast Fact

A whale shark can weigh more than three elephants.

Some fish are **colossal**. This one is more than 50 feet long. Wow!

starry flounder

seahorse

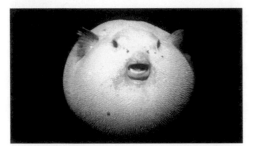

pufferfish

electric eel

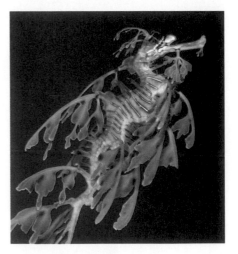

sea dragon

Some fish are as flat as pancakes or as round as balls. Some look like snakes or horses. Some even look like dragons!

But all fish have one thing in common. They are fantastic!

Glossary

colossal (kuh-**loss**-uhl): very big

fin (**fin**): the paddle-shaped part of a fish that is used for moving and steering through the water

freshwater (**fresh**-wa-tur): water that does not contain salt, such as is found in most inland lakes, ponds, and rivers

frigid (**frij**-id): very cold

gill (**gil**): the organ on a fish's side through which it breathes

saltwater (**sawlt**-wa-tur): water that contains salt, such as is found in the ocean

school (**skool**): a group of fish

senses (**sens**-iz): the powers a living thing uses to learn about its environment

Comprehension Questions

1. Can you name three parts of a fish?

2. Can you name five kinds of fish?

3. Which fish in this book is your very favorite? Tell why.